Can You Guess What I Am?
Animals

J.P. Percy

A+

Smart Apple Media

How to use this book

This book combines the fun of a guessing game with some simple information about the variety of animal life.

Start by guessing
- Carefully study the picture on the right-hand page.
- Decide what you think it might be, using both the picture and the clue.
- Turn the page and find out if you are right.

Don't stop there
- Read the extra information about the animal on the following page.
- Turn the page back—did you miss some interesting details?

Enjoy guessing and learning
- Don't worry if you guess wrong—
  everyone does sometimes.
- Your "guessing" will get better
  the more you learn.

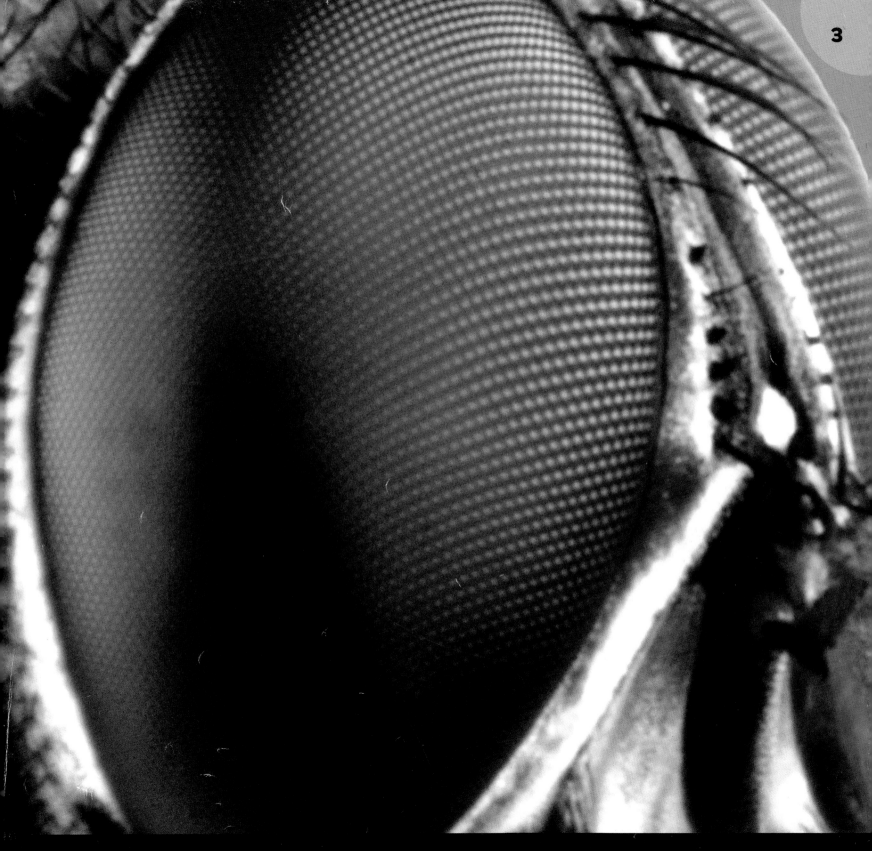

My eyes are nearly as big as my head. Can you guess what I am?

4

I am a fly!

A fly's eye is made up of thousands of tiny parts. They are very good at seeing movement, which is why they are so hard to catch.

My wings are as colorful as the flowers I fly through. Can you guess what I am?

I am a butterfly!

Butterfly wings have lots of tiny scales that overlap. This monarch butterfly's bright wings warn off animals that want to eat it.

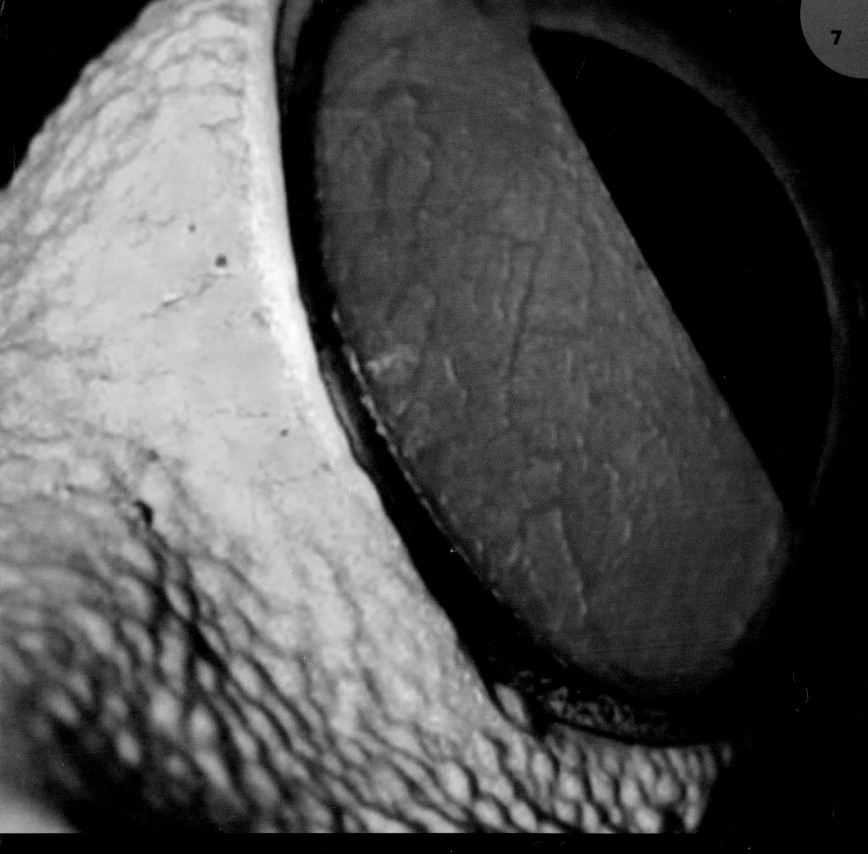

You might see my eyes sticking up out of a pond. Can you guess what I am?

I am a frog!

Frogs can pull their eyes into their head! This helps them to swallow their dinner. It pushes their food into their stomach.

My whiskers may twitch when you stroke me. Can you guess what I am?

I am a cat!

Cats' whiskers help them hunt in the dark. They use their whiskers to pick up smells in the air and sense the shape and size of things around them.

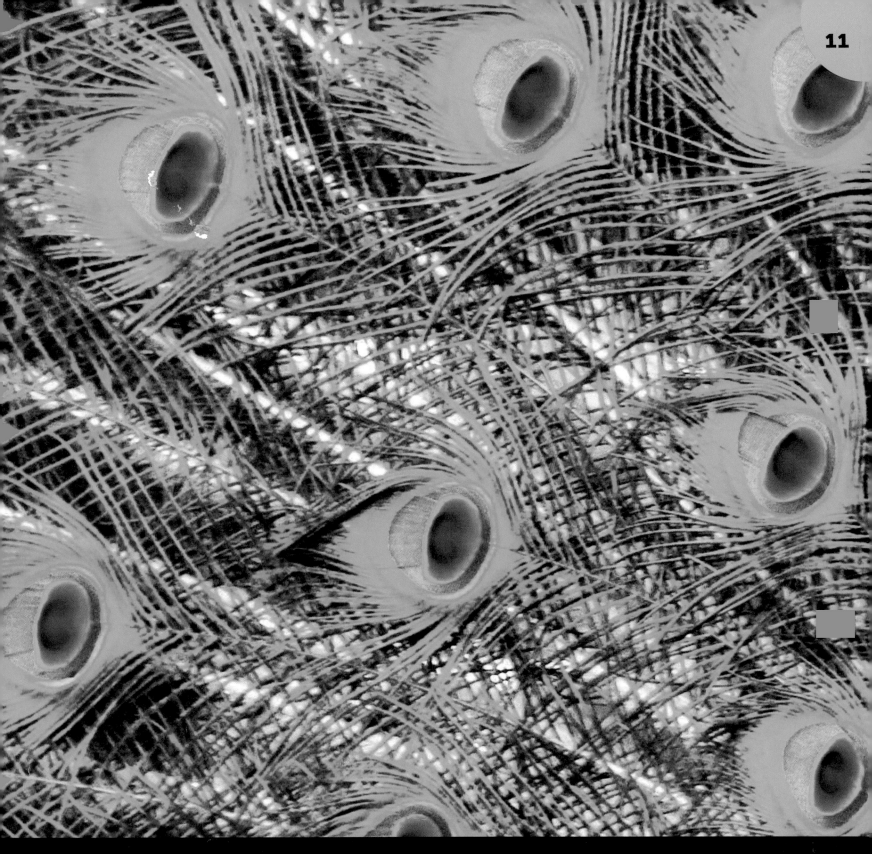

My colorful feathers make sure everyone notices me. Can you guess what I am?

I am a Peacock!

Peacocks have huge, brightly colored tail feathers that they show off to impress peahens. They are one of the largest flying birds in the world.

My skin isn't slimy as you might think. Can you guess what I am?

I am a snake!

Snake skin is usually smooth and dry. It is covered in scales that allow it to grip surfaces. A snake will shed its whole skin many times during its life.

My stripes help me hide in the grasslands of Africa. Can you guess what I am?

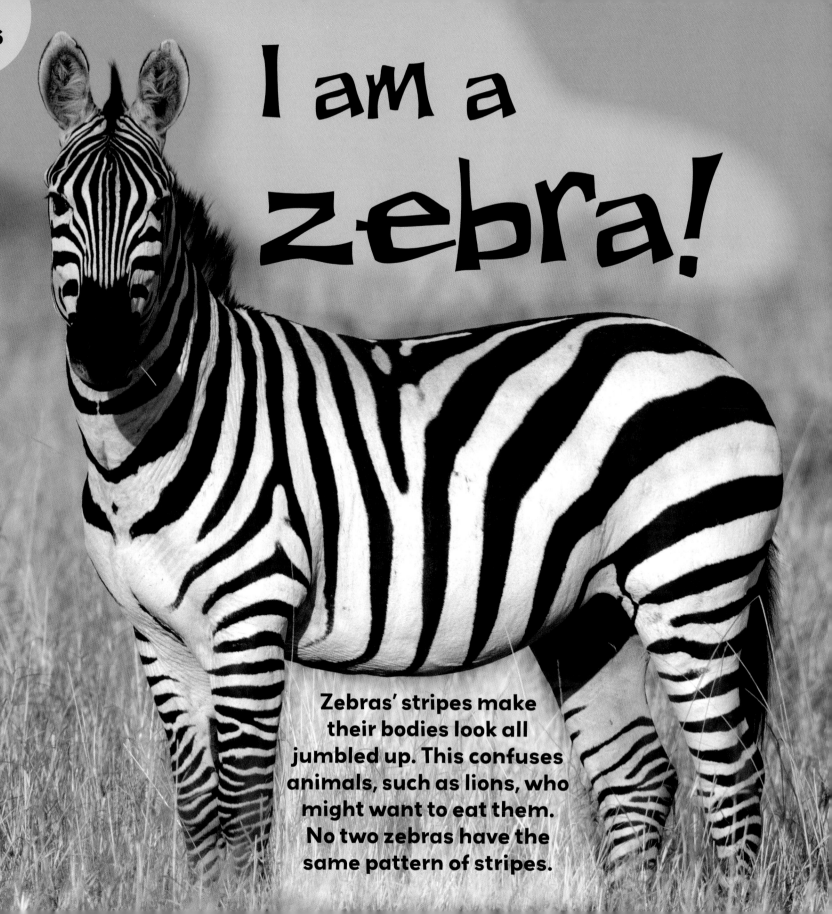

I am a zebra!

Zebras' stripes make their bodies look all jumbled up. This confuses animals, such as lions, who might want to eat them. No two zebras have the same pattern of stripes.

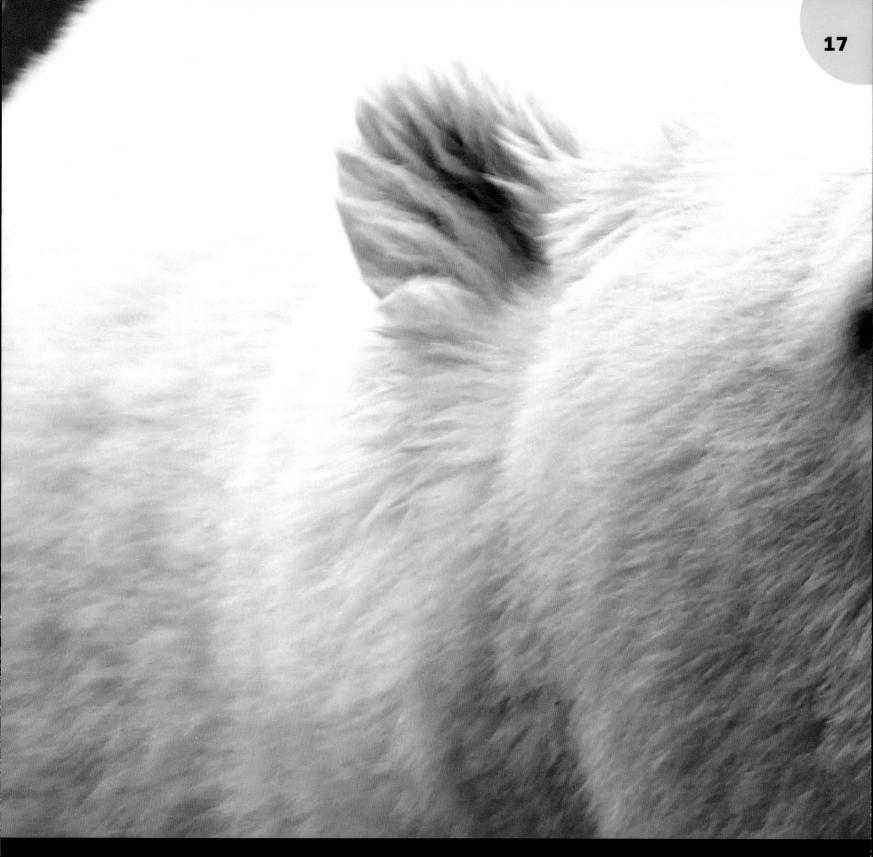

I'm big and furry. I live in the ice and snow. Can you guess what I am?

I am a Polar bear!

Polar bear fur isn't really white—it's see-through! It looks white because it reflects light. The skin under their fur is black. This keeps them warm.

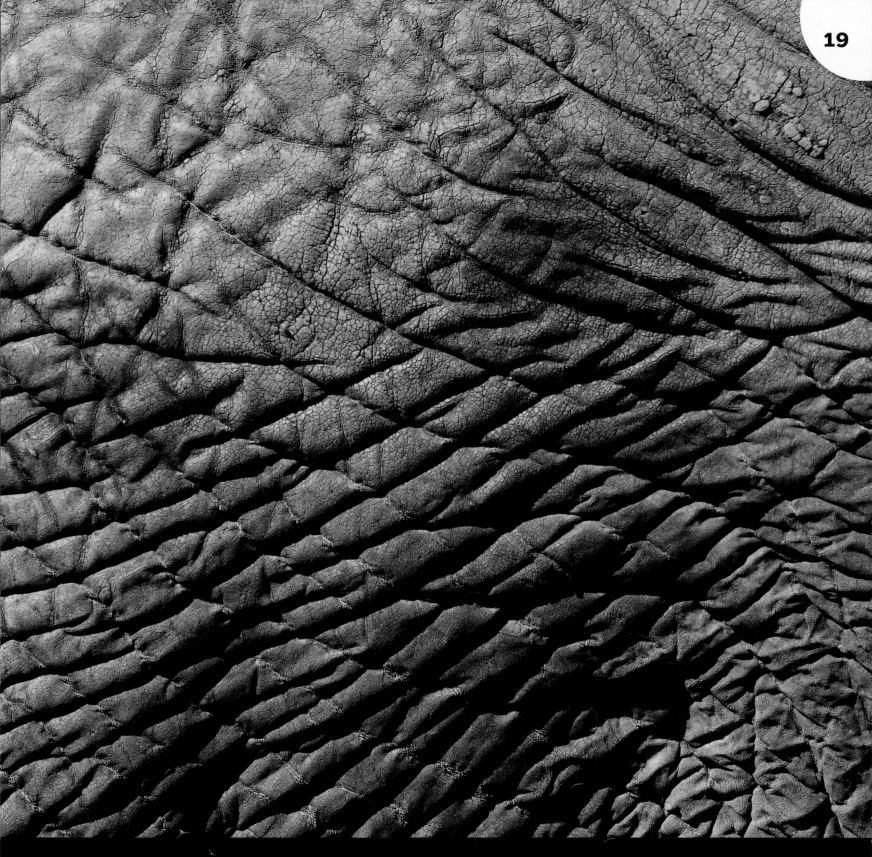

My ears are huge and my skin is very wrinkly. Can you guess what I am?

I am an elephant!

African elephants live in hot countries. Their skin is thick but very sensitive. They roll in mud to protect it from the sun. They also flap their huge ears to help them keep cool.

Now try this...

Make it!
Take a really close look at an animal —or a picture of an animal—and choose a small part to focus on. Then make a picture of that part for people to guess what the animal is. You could look at patterns, or perhaps use scraps of paper or material to make a collage.

Mix it!
Take a large picture of an animal and cut it into smaller pieces to make a jigsaw puzzle. Remember—the more pieces you have, the harder your puzzle will be!

Write it!
Think of your favorite animal. It could be a pet or a wild animal. Think about what makes your animal special—a lion has sharp claws and a dog has a waggy tail. Write a short poem about your chosen animal.

Published by Smart Apple Media, an imprint of Black Rabbit Books
P.O. Box 3263, Mankato, Minnesota 56002
www.blackrabbitbooks.com

Published by arrangement with the Watts Publishing Group LTD, London.

Library of Congress Cataloging-in-Publication Data
Percy, J. P.
 Animals / J.P. Percy.
    pages cm. — (Can you guess what I am?)
 Summary: "Read the clue and carefully look at the picture to guess which animal is pictured in the close-up photograph. Turn the page to find out if you're right and to learn more about the animal!"—Provided by publisher.
 Audience: Grade: K to grade 3.
 ISBN 978-1-59920-892-3 (library binding)
 1. Animals—Juvenile literature. I. Title.
 QL49.P383 2013
 590—dc23
                    2012030848

Series editor: Amy Stephenson
Art director: Peter Scoulding

Picture Credits:
Hintau Aliaksel/Shutterstock: 11, 12. Michael Bielher/Shutterstock: 3. Alex James Bramwell/Shutterstock: front cover tl, 5, 6. Richard Fitzer/Shutterstock: 13. Ian Grainger/Shutterstock: 4. lunatic67/Shutterstock: 14. Marcel Moolj/Shutterstock: 2, 22. moritorus/Shutterstock: front cover tr, 9, 10. Andries Oberholzer/Shutterstock: 19. oversnap/istockphoto: 21. Bernard Richter/Shutterstock: 17, 18. Mogens Trolle/Shutterstock: 15, 16. Vladislav Turchenko/Dreamstime: front cover bl. winterling/istockphoto: front cover br. worldswildlifewonders/Shutterstock: 7, 8.

Every attempt has been made to clear copyright. Should there be any inadvertent omission please apply to the publisher for rectification.

Printed in the United States of America at Corporate Graphics in North Mankato, Minnesota
PO1586
2-2013

9 8 7 6 5 4 3 2 1